POLICY SNACKS

NOSHING YOUR WAY TO POLITICAL SUCCESS

JOHN THIBAULT

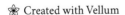 Created with Vellum

DISCLAIMER

Please watch this YouTube video.
Change a Law
Visit Facebook Fan Page

CONTENTS

PREFACE

This book is not about food.

This book is about taking small bites of thought related to politics and policy. Essentially it is a series of articles that, hopefully, will stimulate you to think more not only about the differences and distinctions between policy and politics but also ways that you, the average voter, or small business person can become more engaged, empowered and civic-minded and get a higher taste of what policy can do for you.

I want to whet your appetite and make you realize the hunger you feel, the emptiness inside can sometimes be relieved, not by eating more, but by thinking more and taking an active interest in improving your community.

When we contribute, we have a sense of purpose. When we help others, we attain meaning in our life. When we solve wicked problems, we feel a sense of accomplishment. And when we work with others as a team to achieve these goals, we attain a genuine understanding of the meaning of community and our place in the world.

Sounds like too much to bite off? Well, this buffet of ideas is not meant to satisfy everybody but for the few enlightened souls who genuinely believe there is more to life than competing to meet your own personal needs.

If this resonates with you, then I would love to hear from you, and I hope somewhere somehow this begins to spark a renewed interest and passion for public policy.

John Thibault
    Founder, CEO iLobby
    Menlo Park, CA June 2018

POLITICS IS BORING, TRUST ME ON THIS

I hate politics. I don't understand Congress. And I have no idea about who to vote for in the election." That's what I used to say until the political gene turned on in my late 30's.

For me, politics was boring, and nobody cared. Congress was just a bunch of guys in Washington, and they were going to do whatever they wanted to anyway. Besides, it didn't affect me.

SO MY POSITION was I'd just vote for the candidate who seemed like a rock star and had the best curb appeal. The media and the Party would make sure I picked the right one.

But in 1990, I started a new job working in Governmental Affairs at MCA/Universal, and things changed. Daily, we were dealing with public policy issues, and I soon realized there were three words I had left out of my former simple political assessment; issues, resources, and outcomes.

So if you plug these three words in, the formula suddenly changes. Politics isn't dull. It's about issues.

Congress isn't a bunch of faceless people. It's a machine for allocating resources and setting the rules. And elections aren't about celebrity stardom. Elections have outcomes.

Once I understood that the election altered resource allocation and this affected the actual issues in my life, it became clear that Washington policy decisions transform the political arena from a boring collection of stuffy politicians into a rich landscape of diverse human opinions struggling with complex problems and many constituents.

Why did MCA think politics was important?

According to the L.A. Times, "It was (Lew) Wasserman's bitter experience with that deal (consent decree of 1959) that made him realize the importance of political clout, causing him to become a voracious fund-raiser and student of the political scene." [1]

I must have picked up on this in the time we were in his office talking about our PAC.

When I was at MCA, I realized the company had issues, but I did not. The company had resources while I had few. MCA/Universal desired legislative outcomes that would continue to protect and enhance their resources. Think copyright protection, anti-piracy for music and film, union issues, etc. For the company, elections were about supporting the politicians aligned with their problems.

So we remained very close to world leaders, Congress, and every administration since the Kennedy administration.

You might say that large corporations have political interests they want to protect. And that's exactly right. But so do small businesses and individuals. So why are we so much less involved?

For individuals, I think one key factor is a lack of resources. In a way, this goes back to the same political gene I mentioned earlier. Until you have something at stake, you don't really care. When you get married, or you have children, or you start a small business or lose a division of your company, then you start paying attention.

Big companies are paying attention all the time. That's why they have a dominant influence in Congress, and they hire lobbyists to represent them. They have the discretionary resources (time, money, and staff) to allocate, focus their concerns, and protect their interests.

We shouldn't blame them for that. Otherwise, we might not have the rich diversity of products and services we use every day at a price we are accustomed to.

Yet, as individuals, we believe we do not have sufficient resources. Therefore we don't engage in politics. We also mistakenly think the system is so corrupt or ineffective, there is nothing we can do.

So we resign ourselves to play a simple role. We vote in the general election because it requires the least effort on our part. Strange.

We do the least and expect the most, yet we condemn those who succeed. Still, we won't take part in the political arena.

But if we could find a way to simplify politics, understand the issues that affect us, and muster collective resources, we might want to claim a more significant part in the game. We would have some control, autonomy, and capacity because that's what we need.

That's what grassroots politics is all about. But somehow even that sounds boring. Why? Because it doesn't deal with "My Issue." So what is my issue?

First, we need to ask how does this legislation affect me? And the answer is not, "It doesn't."

The exciting thing is that while you may not care about politics, other people do. Your silence and non-participation mean that other people will decide how things go in your life. So if you like to be told what to do and how to live your life, then sit back and enjoy the bumpy, frustrating ride.

Ignore the issues, keep voting for the same incumbent politicians, never measure their performance, don't involve yourself in any problems you care about, and do not connect the dots.

Apathy begets apathy.

Indolence begets indolence. And ignorance begets ignorance.

Stop paying attention for another few election cycles, and in 10 years you won't recognize who you are or what country you are living in.

Then ask yourself again. Is politics still boring?

-----

[1] Bates, J. (2002, June 04). The Hollywood Mogul and Kingmaker

Dies at 89 LEW R. WASSERMAN: 1913 - 2002 Legacy: As MCA chief, his behind-the-scenes clout guided an industry and extended to politics. Retrieved from Los Angeles Times.

WHY SMALL BUSINESS SHOULD LOBBY

When persuading lawmakers to simplify regulations or adopt legislation, you are fighting for, as a small business, you face three choices.

- You can sit on the sidelines
- You can petition
- You can lobby

MOST SMALL BUSINESSES CHOOSE #1. You do nothing. You grumble and complain because you feel like you can't do anything.

The second option; you join an organization or trade association focused on a single industry or issue. You pay dues, sign petitions, and promote your cause through the organization, whether you agree with them or not.

You could also try the third choice. If you are lucky enough to grow to a sufficient size and have adequate resources, you can put a toe in the water and hire a PR firm, public affairs staff, or a lobbyist, often with mixed results. You realize you are a small fish in a big pond, and lobbying is a complicated and expensive undertaking when you do it alone.

So how can you cut through the red tape and get the regulations you want?

To lobby effectively, you need three basic fundamentals:

- Control
- Constituents
- Capacity

CONTROL

SITTING it out provides no benefits. You already know that.

But working with an active industry group offers some comfort. However, you sacrifice control of your message, the campaign, and you delegate execution into the hands of the organization.

By hiring your own PR firm or staff, you preserve full message or issue control, but it's expensive. You need deep pockets, and there is no guarantee of satisfactory results.

CONSTITUENTS

EVERYBODY NEEDS constituents or supporters (i.e., voters). If you don't plead your case and convince others to join you, nothing will happen. That's a given. But if you persuade people one at a time through word of mouth, this can take a long time.

The exception occurs when your cause is built on passion and strong public support. Think MADD, Amber Alerts, and Jessica's Law.

If you join a group like the local business council or single-issue non-profit, other constituents believe in the same thing you do. You may not get to know very many of the other members, and more substantial interests can take precedence, while geography will limit contact.

Large corporations and special interests represent a large constituent base, but you have to ask yourself. Can they really cajole all their employees or members to vote the way management wants? Probably not. So they may have phantom constituents and lawmakers know this. Lawmakers respond to real voters, but they have to be singular in focus, and there has to be a lot of them.

Capacity

If your company has limited discretionary resources, then you won't have the financial capacity to undertake long term lobbying. So it is difficult to make a lot of legislative progress. But if you join a professional or trade association, you can increase your chances of success.

Large corporations and special interests, on the other hand, have relatively unlimited resources, which gives them staying power. They understand the economic and political benefit of applying those resources to correcting any laws that impact their business or regulations that impede their interests.

So having surveyed the landscape, how can a small businessman compete and lobby successfully?

The Ideal Solution

Let's say you want to get a law passed, or regulation changed. You want to control the issue, have broad support from real voters, and you want to contain costs. Finally, you don't want to spend 100% of your time in Washington or city hall.

So how do you attain autonomy, support, and low cost?

If your current political plan isn't working, then you need to find a new way.

You can craft your message. You can control the debate and find the best arguments to support your cause through crowdsourcing. You can reach supporters, customers, and suppliers around the country who have similar interests. You can lower costs by sharing the lobbying expense with a broad group of people.

With these three elements: control, constituents, and capacity, you can overcome bureaucratic inertia and your legislative limitations.

You identify the Congressman who sits on the Committee related to your issue. With voters from many different Congressional districts simultaneously approaching their representatives on the same singular issue, all coordinated in one campaign by one lobbyist, (almost like a symphony), you gain incredible, surgical precision and political power. And that's what you want.

Just like with your business, you need to focus, take control and work with other small companies passionately convincing them to join you to implement the fresh new ideas and legislative solutions that you want to happen.

Lift the regulatory burden, but ask your friends and business associates to help. It takes more than voting. Political engagement needs to be part of your ongoing daily business strategy. And that's why small businesses should lobby.

3 WAYS OF GETTING WHAT YOU WANT

There are three ways of getting what you want in almost every area of life. You can petition, you can protest, or you can persuade. Can it really be that simple? Sure. Take a look.

3 Ways

1. Petition
2. Protest
3. Persuade

Petition

ASK NICELY.

To get what you want, you have to ask for it. Most of us know what we don't want and have a vague idea of what we do want. But we never really ask. Or we are afraid to. Why? Because when we ask, we often fear our request will be denied, and we'll be disappointed.

Sometimes you're afraid to ask for something on your own. You need help. So you get people's agreement, their signatures, and you hope that if you have more support, the likelihood is that you will be granted this thing you are asking for.

Petitioners are on the positive side of the ledger. You ask for what you want, you hope you can get it, and when you ask you learn that if you have more people to help you, it will increase your chances of success.

There is also a subtle threat that if you are rejected, you will tell more people about what you're asking for and whether or not you receive it, and often politicians and corporations will cave-in to mass petitions and grant the request, sometimes grudgingly.

Protest

Demand aggressively.

The negative side of asking is demanding. A negative request is a protest. You immediately take a confrontational point of view. You don't ask. You tell. You don't request it. You demand.

Protestors create demonstrations and boycotts. They are very public about what they were doing. They gain followers. They have short slogans. They sometimes break things, and that is their way of acting out and yelling to get what they want. Protesters become quite emotional and active.

Like a spoiled child, there are implicit threats that if they don't get what they want, they will pout, throw a temper tantrum, or worse. Yes, even grownups do this.

Often people don't know what the protestor wants. Protestors don't always have a clear message and frustrated, they can become violent.

Does it work? Sometimes.

In the end, their wish is sometimes granted, but usually at a high cost.

Some people think that if they have tried both, asking and protesting, and they get a "no" each time, that's an invitation to ask again. Salesmen do this all the time. They love rejection. This is the beginning of our 3rd way, persuasion.

PERSUADE

CONVINCE INTELLIGENTLY.

Most of us don't know how to effectively convince others. If we go it alone, our plea may not carry enough weight. But when we join a crowd, we act like a mob, and that doesn't work.

Part of this is that we simply have not thought the process through.

We may not like to use persuasion, we're not great orators, and we're not comfortable in the role of the salesperson.

I would like to suggest that personal persuasion is a hybrid form and a more elegant way than either of the former two ways and should become your number one conviction strategy for getting what you want.

You see, when you petition, you are expecting someone to give you something. When you protest, you are demanding it. But when you persuade, you are giving something first and showing how the other party will benefit by coming around to your way of thinking.

The best dealmakers are often charismatic and very good at persuasion.

Persuading is subtle. It is about relationship building. It is about forming coalitions. It is about convincing others how everyone can benefit from some wise plan that you initiate.

It is not selfish. It represents the height of diplomacy.

So the next time you want something huge and important, like a new job, an investment in your business, a home loan, a marriage proposal, a new law -- don't ask, don't threaten... but persuade.

Figure out how the vision you have will benefit the most people, share it, and find like-minded people who will then bend over backward to help make your dreams come true.

Persuade eloquently.

You may be surprised by what you get.

7 STEPS TO POLITICAL EMPOWERMENT

If you feel overwhelmed and frustrated by our government leaders and apathetic about your own partisan destiny, there is a way out of your political malaise.

Here are 7 simple steps you can take to refresh yourself and participate in our democratic republic.

7 STEPS

1. Register
2. Learn
3. Vote
4. Commit
5. Engage
6. Lobby
7. Run

1. Register to vote

. . .

SHOW UP. There are 45 million unregistered eligible voters in the country. Don't be one of them. If you're eligible to vote, register. 215 million US voters can't be wrong. Locate the registrar of voters in your state or county. Fill in the form.

TIP: An absentee ballot makes things simple and easy.
   Time: 1-hour Frequency: Once Cost: Free [1]

2. Learn

GET INFORMED AND STAY INFORMED. Find out who your congressman is, your assemblyman, your senators, your mayor. Go to their websites. Get on their email lists and follow their progress. Follow other political websites. Read political and opinion articles in major respected newspapers, listen to talk radio, watch cable, and network TV debates.

TIP: Compare and contrast information sources.
   Time: 4 hours Frequency: Once a year Cost: $50

3. Vote

MAKE A DECISION. Choose. Vote in every election you qualify for. Read the campaign materials and gather independent non-partisan information. Read the candidates' statements, so you are as informed as possible. Then vote. Vote for the best candidate, not the ticket, not the party. Remember, voting is private. If you have an absentee ballot, you can vote ahead of Election Day without looking for a polling station or disrupting your life.

Tip: Think for yourself.
  Time: 2 hours Frequency: Every 2 years Cost: Free

4. Commit

Put your money where your mouth is. Make a small donation to your Congressman's campaign. $5-20 is fine. If you believe in what he is doing, support his campaign. If you don't, support the opponent or challenger. Remember, donations are public information. Follow the rules.

Tip: Donate small amounts to several candidates.
  Time: 1-hour Frequency: Every 2 years Cost: $20

5. Engage

Take a stand. Engage where you are. Identify the laws you want to change. Talk to your friends. Then convince others to join you. Comment on a blog and sign a petition to support a cause or issue. Write to your representative and voice your opinion. Attend a town hall meeting. Attend city council meetings or a fundraiser. Serve on a local committee. Volunteer to help out on a campaign. Visit city hall, your state capital, or Washington DC. Take a tour. Ask questions.

Tip: Volunteer, but only if you enjoy it.

Time: 2 hours Frequency: Every 3 months Cost: Free

6. Lobby

BUILD A COALITION. Start by focusing on the top three issues that personally affect you. Write up your topic, your position, your arguments, and your facts. Resolve your position, clarify your arguments, and win support from your network. Expand your base, increase your reach, and share the cost.

You can lead it on your own.

Lobbying used to be only for the rich, powerful, and connected. But now anyone can do it. Grassroots activism does not require you to join a single-issue organization, a trade association, pay union dues, or contribute to a PAC.

You can drive costs down by sharing resources and costs with thousands of other people focused around a single common issue. With increased purchasing power, you can have the same influence as a special interest.

The benefits will include less time, less money, greater mobility, ubiquity, increased control, and getting laws changed. Every day, everywhere, lobby on the go.

TIP: Be honest and straightforward, and you'll be amazed at your results.

Time: 15 min. Frequency: Monthly Cost: $25

7. Run

. . .

LEAD. The world needs leaders. Run for office. Now that you've learned a lot and decided that you're tired of someone less competent controlling the agenda, you should run for office.

If you are willing to serve and help other people, then you will find that this is something that will become your life. You will want to do it all the time.

You will know this is for you because you listen to your supporters, you have the facts about solving real-world problems, and you can implement policy solutions.

At this point, you will know if you have the political bug or not.

If you have issues, and friends and family that support you, then this could be your ticket to political empowerment. Charisma and excellent speaking skills can come later.

Once you are in, there'll be many people to help you to the next level. Good luck.

TIP: Don't stay in longer than you need to.
Time: 8 hours Frequency: Daily Cost: $5,000+

-----

[1] All estimates of the time required, frequency, and cost are minimums only.

CONGRESS DESERVES D BUT MY CONGRESSMAN GETS AN A+

A ccording to a recent poll [1], the job performance rating of Congress continues to reflect a meager 7% positive job approval score. Why is that?

Why do we accept such poor performance? Do we think if they did more, worked harder, longer, smarter, they'd get a better result?

Do we want Congress to be more productive and pass more laws with more pages? Even now, we learn that Dodd-Frank has 5,320 pages covering 400 new regulations [2]. Obama Care was a 2,700-page bill, and so far has 13,000 pages of new regulations [3]. Or do we want Congress to undo some of the old laws that we no longer like? Would we prefer Congress to respond to issues that we think are important? Or did we elect our members to vote the way he or she wants?

If the polls are right, and 90% of Americans believe that Congress is doing a poor job, how can that be? Are we accepting mediocrity as the price of freedom? If we vote for the "best candidate" in our district, why are they so effective campaigning as a candidate and so ineffective as a Member of Congress?

Have campaigning and fundraising proficiency trumped their legislative ability?

Ask yourself, why do we keep electing the same politicians if we get inferior results year after year?

Is it because Congress is not performance-based?

We know it is not a meritocracy. The best do not rise to the top. The best are not rewarded for their excellent behavior. Seniority rules. So incumbency attracts power. Power attracts position and campaign donations. Then position and donations are used to attract more support, votes, and tenure.

Maybe we're using the wrong metrics when we think about measuring Congress' job performance.

If the pollsters are right and Congress is as bad as they claim, then each of us is responsible for continuing to elect poor performers to the Congress. Or are they accomplished people who are incapable of getting anything done because they have to continually convince a majority of their 535 peers?

Whenever I have seen voters with their Congressman, they are always gushing, the voters, not the Congressmen. They refuse to ask tough questions. They throw politically convenient softballs, which the Congressman always has the answer to, or he makes sure he can use artful circumlocution to wend his way out of a messy question.

Constituents inevitably are very polite. They invite their friends to fundraisers. They are delighted to contribute to the campaign. They seem to be happy with a photo-op standing next to power. And they vote for the same politician over and over and over again.

But when the polls come out, voters polled turn and complain that Congress is not doing its job. Well, which is it? They are the doing the job we elected them to do, or they are incompetent, economically illiterate, politically mendacious boobs?

If we look at Congress as a whole, it may only be as strong as its weakest link. So, we need to identify the poor performers. They need to be voted out of office.

In corporate America, on an annual basis, some companies cull 5%-10% of their lowest-performing workforce. But if we did that, can we expect superior performance from the entire body of Congress? Not if we keep electing the same incumbents for 5, 10, or 15 terms?

I'm not advocating term limits here, as some states currently have. This sometimes has the unintended consequence of taking good, seasoned politicians and pushing them out of office.

But if we had a way to systematically look at the Members of Congress, compare them one to the other on an independent basis and discover who falls into the bottom third, it should make it easy to figure out who should then not be reelected.

Political party strategists focus on this, but even weak performing incumbents with name recognition can still draw sufficient contributions to drown out a challenger's voice.

So instead of supporting our congressmen and blindly awarding him an A+ and then complain about the body of Congress by giving them a D-, we should examine carefully who our Congressman is and ask a different set of questions.

What is my representative's position on the issues that matter to me, and what legislation has he sponsored? What committees or subcommittees does he chair? How much did he receive from his Party committee, the DNC, the RNC, etc.? Who are his big donors? What percentage of his financial support came from outside his state?

It might surprise you to learn that your district votes may be heavily influenced by media buys sometimes financed by out of state interests.[4] Someone wants you to vote for the incumbent, so you don't rock the boat. Who benefits from his incumbency?

What success has your representative had? What has he done for you? What are his key issues, and are his actions really improving your community, your business, your neighborhood, and your congressional district?

So if your representative deserves an A, give it to him, but don't tell the pollsters Congress deserves a D.

Unless you are politically engaged, you may never understand how Congress earns a D while your Congressman always gets an A.

As Thomas Jefferson said, "We in America do not have government by the majority. We have government by the majority who participate."

So engage politically, and give your Congressman an honest grade.

-----

[1] Rasmussen, S. (2012, 13-Jul). Election 2012 - Congressional Performance. From Rasmussen Reports

[2] Harper, J. (2012, May 07). Inside the Beltway: Dodd-Frank=5,320 pages. Retrieved from Washington Times

[3] York, B. (2012, 29-March). Washington Examiner. From Obamacare's 2,700 pages are too much for justices

[4] Megahy, F. (Writer), & Megahy, F. (Director). (2009). The Best Government Money Can Buy [Motion Picture].

GET MONEY OUT OF POLITICS NOW

We should get money out of politics. Everyone says it is corrosive and corrupts.

But ask any candidate who lost his last campaign if he could have used more money and I think he'll say yes.

The problem is not too much money. The problem is narrowly focused sources of cash. Narrow cash doesn't work. In plain English, narrowly focused funding sources empower special interests.

In one sense, we don't like special interests because we are not part of the group. But if we were, we would ignore our own hypocrisy and cheer for our 1st Amendment rights.

There's probably an algorithm for the correct balance of financial breadth and depth and its political influence.

You want more of the former (breadth) and less of the latter (depth).

That's why candidates prefer small political donations, but they know they are challenging to deal with. So they also like bundlers. Bundlers give the appearance of bringing in smaller donations, but the candidate only has to deal with a few people who take credit for the contribution and get the privilege of presenting their position on issues as if they represented everyone who passed money through them.

But getting the right mix of broad support, small donations, and sufficient capital to cover a campaign that addresses a range of representative views remains a delicate balancing act.

Money doesn't come just from special interests, large corporations, lobbyists, and unions. It can also come from other congressmen and committees (RNC, DNC, DSCC) who have been oversubscribed and can pass funding to those candidates who support the party line.

The public doesn't hear much about this.

So, the key is not to get rid of money in politics. I think that's almost impossible.

Politicians need to reach their constituents at election time, and the cost of doing this gets higher every year. If the media wanted to give every candidate free airtime, free radio time, and free space, that would reduce the cost for the campaign. But then mass media companies wouldn't be running a business, would they?

It's awkward. You give money to your representative to get the word out. He pays a network for airtime. You watch TV and believe the 15-second spot, and you vote for him. The only one out-of-pocket is you.

So my opinion is not to support public financing of campaigns (broad) nor is it doing away with special interests (narrow).

It's not all or nothing. It rarely is.

What the voter wants is for his representative to listen to him anyway, but this is not guaranteed by a small donation or by a vote.

I think small donors need to become politically engaged. They must step up to the plate. They need to find a way to collectively express their opinions so that they gain the advantage of representing views that really matter to them.

If individual voters could come together as a group in an ad-hoc way over issues that matter to them, they could quickly gain the funding power of a large corporation, union, or special interest and hire lobbyists to represent them. It's a novel idea but completely doable.

You don't have to contribute to a candidate's campaign. After all, it is rare that your congressman would hold similar views to every one of yours. Instead, you commit to an idea, a cause that becomes a piece of legislation.

If just 2,000 people across the country (1/10 of 1% of all voters), agreed to give $25 a month, that would be $50,000 ($600,000 per year) that could go to advocating for a specific issue. Looking at the numbers, you realize it wouldn't take much for the public to take an aggressive stance and really push an agenda forward, effectively competing for the first time on an equal footing with the more giant, powerful corporations and other entrenched special interests.

Or maybe $25 is too much to ask, and instead, we should keep paying for coffee, cable, and concerts. Special interests understand that democracy is not free. It's time you and I put not just our 2 cents in, but also our voice, our cash, and our commitment. Or we can sit around grumbling for another four years while the political cycle whirls around us and empties our pockets.

HOW TO DEBATE

Structurally speaking, a debate has five main parts:

1. Summary
2. Position
3. Arguments
4. Rebuttals
5. Conclusion

MOST DEBATES ALSO HAVE rules about their resources. These serve to act as constraints. They are:

- Time
- Votes

THE PURPOSE of debate is to come to a decision about a complex issue or topic. This is important because once you reach a decision, you're free to take action.

So the debate is really a decision process tool.

Let me break down the five main parts.

1. Summary

THE SUMMARY IS like an opening statement or thesis. It is best if it is open-ended and posed as a question.

In the summary, you pose a question often starting with the word "Should... " i.e., should the US be energy independent? Should Congress audit the Federal Reserve? Should we ban assault weapons? Should bad teachers be fired from our public schools?

You are not trying to build an argument to support your case just yet. At this stage, you're simply asking a question.

The summary usually includes some background or facts to set out the framework for the audience.

2. Position

THE POSITION IS SIMPLE. You either support the thesis (summary), or you oppose it. You are either for it or against it.

Once you know your position, then it is easy to argue. Generally, you will argue on one side of the issue or the other.

3. Arguments

· · ·

BECAUSE PEOPLE often have not made up their minds, you may find when you speak with someone they argue out of both sides of their mouth. This happens because they either don't know their position or don't have the courage of their convictions.

Depending on what side of the fence you're on, you select one side of an issue, and you advance arguments that support your position.

Arguments are intended to convince your audience that you are right, that they should adopt your position, and in that way, you gain support for your central thesis.

Arguing is not yelling. It's persuading. It's not as complicated as it sounds because we do it every day. We just don't realize it, and we don't do it very well.

Your arguments do not come out of thin air. They are generally based on facts. So, you (the proponent) bring facts, reports, witnesses, statistics, or anecdotal evidence to the table to support your case.

The person arguing on the other side (your opponent) will bring conflicting evidence to support their case or point of view.

Visualize this as T and things should fall into place.

4. Rebuttals

To ADD A LITTLE MORE COMPLEXITY, we need to understand the value and placement of rebuttals and counter-rebuttals.

A rebuttal on the support side weakens the main argument. On the other hand, a counter-rebuttal would diminish the strength of the opposition's arguments.

The counter-rebuttal acts as a double negative and could actually support the positive side of the argument, while a rebuttal to the main argument could help the opposition.

Think of debates like competitive sports. Until you pick a team to support, it's not very interesting. But once you get engaged, then you can't wait to see who wins or loses.

. . .

5. Conclusion

THE RESOLUTION of the debate occurs when one side wins. The conclusion leads to a precise outcome, and this determination leads to action.

Let me comment on the two process constraint variables I mentioned.

- Time
- Votes

Time

IN LIVE DEBATE, while time is a resource, it acts as a constraint and restricts how much a debater can spend on any one argument. Theoretically, this sharpens their thinking. And like any game that has a fixed amount of time, a debate can run its course, and then at some predetermined time, the argument is cut off. Political discussions are an excellent example of this.

VOTES

AT THE CONCLUSION, a moderator gives the audience a chance to vote, just as a judge allows a jury to deliberate after a trial.

They may vote based on facts or style. But in the end, the audience inevitably picks one side or the other. They select the winner.

A debate is a competition about ideas and the expression of an idea. All debates have rules. In real-life, debates have moderators to keep the entire process moving along.

If you understand the structure of the debate and the five main components, then it becomes clear how to position your message to convince others about what you want them to believe.

Often when people argue they: a) don't have the facts b) they bull-headedly stick to one side even when they are not sure of what their position is anyway or c) they resort to ad-hominem attacks. You see this all the time on talk radio and cable-TV.

This kind of quasi-debate can become emotional and anarchic. So the participants don't really follow formal rules. In these instances, civil discourse breaks down, there is a failure of diplomacy and violence, and unreasoning asserts itself.

Remember, a debate intends to intelligently resolve complex issues about topics of concern to many people.

Learning to debate does not mean you need to become a great orator or do massive amounts of research.

Learning how to debate simply means you understand what you believe in, you are clear on your position and have a few good arguments to back you up.

So by learning how to debate and following the rules, you can convince others to support you, respect you, and increase your chances of getting what you want.

HOW YOUR TRADE ASSOCIATION CAN HAVE GREATER POLITICAL IMPACT

There are 90,908 trade associations in the country. With philanthropic and charitable organizations, the number rises to over 1.2 million [1]. In any event, there are lots. Every trade association has a dual role: 1) to increase membership and 2) to promote the cause of the organization.

Your association relies on its members and other activities for funding. But it has an untapped and overlooked hidden stream of potential advocates that it could use more effectively.

As a leader of a trade association, you may poll your members to find out what are their top issues. You summarize a select few, and these are the ones you focus on and go forward with. Most organizations are usually single-issue organizations.

Legislatively, you compete with other associations for the time and attention of lobbyists, legislators, congressional staff members, and government regulators. You rely upon your membership numbers and your PAC's campaign giving to support your cause and to gain access to Washington lawmakers.

For the largest organizations, often, this is enough. But for the smaller and midsize groups, they might find themselves struggling to push their agendas forward.

Sometimes, you can rally your membership to take on different activities, but generally, you can't do it that often. Like any group, your members tend to experience what is referred to as "donor fatigue." They don't want to donate more money, they do not wish to donate more time, and they can't take time off work to get on the bus to attend a rally to hold a sign in the pouring rain. While association members as a whole may appreciate the opportunity to vote up or down on issues, they often feel they are left out of the full debate creation and argument process.

So can smart leadership still get them involved?

Sure.

THE BEST ASSOCIATION leaders allow their members four things:

1. To come forward with topics of their own concern.
2. Provide a forum for the members to discuss issues.
3. Allow their membership to respectfully debate arguments pro and con on various sides of a problem.
4. Provide a place where members can vote anonymously.

ESSENTIALLY, they give their members a voice.

The best association leaders also know that family members often influence what the member thinks. The chief lobbyist, it turns out, is often the spouse.

Association leaders recognize that their members are not one-dimensional. They do not have only one issue that matters to them. They may be members of many different special interest groups because several various issues concern them. The member joins different groups that support his cause. So in effect, he could be a member of a pro-gun group, a pro-choice group, a clean energy group, and a business development incubator. He may be a moderate on social issues and conservative or entrepreneur on business issues.

Some political independents that neither lean left nor right fall into this middle category.

But, there remains one highly overlooked element.

Imagine the trade association member is a US voter and a constituent of a congressional district. His alternate issues may span into other congressional districts. In the district they span into may reside friends and associates who support the nature of your particular membership group. But the voter in the other region is not and cannot be a member of your trade association because he simply is in a different profession or geographical area.

So how do you cross the line? Can you take advantage of this? I think you can.

If your trade association members were free to openly debate and vote anonymously in a safe, independent, non-partisan environment, the likelihood is great that they would continue to support your efforts. After all, they are in your business. And if their spouse and friends from other states were able to share in a debate, then they too could bring more significant weight to your argument and causes.

But more importantly, all these interested parties are constituents in other political districts. If they can lobby their congressman or representative who may sit on crucial Congressional committees that affect your broader issue, then you could bring a greater force to bear by empowering more people to push legislation forward that supports and benefits your organization.

Can this be done? Certainly.

Let's say your association allocates $25,000 per year to lobby or about $2,000 a month.

If an additional 2,000 voters from 10 different districts contributed $20 a month to support your efforts, you would have $40,000 a month extra for lobbying or almost a half-million dollars a year. If these voters were aligned with your cause and made their issues known to their congressman, your impact could increase twenty-fold at no real out-of-pocket cost to you or your association.

. . .

THE MOST SIGNIFICANT impacts any independent constituent group can have are:

1. Clarity of message and singular focus on an issue.
2. Mass of voters who can appeal to the Congress.
3. A real budget to continue and persevere.

REMEMBER, these are real voters and Congress loves to hear from its own constituents.

So, the advocate is not a nameless organization supporting a large, broad membership that may or may not support its overall goals. Working together through social networks, you now have real people putting up their own money to support causes, which are aligned with your organization's needs.

Because voters will have self-identified as constituents to congressional members on committees affecting your organization, your impact in Washington with lawmakers will increase.

Encourage your members to pursue their interests and make public their issues and you may find that your best ally could well be, not just your association member, but also her family and network of friends.

-----

[1] The Center for Association Leadership

JUST WAIT TILL NOVEMBER

Many of us are frustrated and annoyed by the hypocrisy and infighting in Washington. We are constantly reminded that elections have consequences, and November is our time to act at the ballot box.

All of this is true, but I know many of us remain antsy. So can we do more?

If you think things are dysfunctional at the federal level, you should try the state and local city councils. I think you'll find the same.

When we are told we should get together with our friends and neighbors to pursue issues that we have in common and voice our concern, this is true. But often we don't know our real neighbors. Because of this, our friends and neighbors have become our new virtual friends and neighbors in online communities and blogs. This separation makes it difficult to pursue collective action.

We mistakenly think that if we vote for the President of our choice, all our ills will be cured when he gets into office. We also believe that he is the perfect embodiment and representative of all the issues that we are concerned about, and he is taking the right stance on those issues.

So between now and November, we watch only those political spots that support our candidate for President, and we ignore the rest, or we bash them in a self-gratifying way. We think of this election season like a horse race. Will our guy win? Place and show are irrelevant.

But our President and even our representatives are not the sole embodiment of all the issues that we agree with.

If you wanted to have a meeting with the President about an issue of utmost importance to you, the likelihood of that happening is almost nil. If, on the other hand, you wanted to have a discussion with your Congressmen in your district about an issue that concerns you, the likelihood of having that meeting is considerably higher.

Since it is within Congress where legislation is formed, it is probably better for you to devote your time to get to know your elected representatives, your Congressman and your Senators. But going a step beyond that is also doubtless really good for your political well-being.

First, figure out what your top three or five issues are, what your position is, and where you stand on these issues.

After all, it is all about issues. It is not about the personality or the charisma of the politician. Ultimately politics is about issues. In a democracy, issues are problems that get debated on and later get resolved through laws.

When a President issues an Executive Order, he doesn't consult with you or your representative about what he wants to put into law. He just does it.[1]

So much for your presidential vote!

But to be even blunter, your vote for President is the popular vote, and it doesn't really count anyway. At least not the way you think.

The President is put into office by the Electoral College[2], not by you. Members of the Electoral College are selected and pledge allegiance to the presidential candidate of their choice, and they vote accordingly.

So unless you are a delegate to the convention and an elector, you should probably focus on your district representatives with whom you have more influence.

But to come back to my earlier point, you don't just call them up, write them, try to meet at their office, or speak up at a Townhall meeting unless you know what you're talking about. You don't know what you're talking about unless you have an understanding of key issues affecting you and your district.

So, look at the top five things that are causing you harm. List the five things that you think need to be changed. Delve into these issues and find out more. See which side of the matter you stand on.

Then you can actively participate in the political process, well beyond voting.

You don't need to wait till November. You don't need to keep silent for two years in a row, then vote and keep silent again for another two years.

You can find like-minded people now. You can clarify your thoughts and your message now. You can attain the persistence of vision, pursue issue advocacy, and help change things to improve your community, your state, and the country.

Voter turnout generally remains low. Political activism among the middle-class or the silent majority ("non-special interests") is even smaller.

So it should come as no surprise that those who have a clear message, know their position, have enough grassroots community support and money to pursue their issue are the ones who get their legislation passed. And they do this quietly, persistently and they do this every day.

They also vote at election time. But they don't let the election prevent them from taking action now.

So my message is this. Don't focus on politicians or parties. Focus on issues.

Don't wait till November. Take action now.

Don't do this in isolation. Join with other people who believe in and support your issue. And finally, pool your strengths and resources and work with professionals to pursue your cause.

-----

[1] Archives, National. (2012, March 20). Federal Register Executive Orders. Retrieved March 20, 2012, from Executive Orders Disposition Tables - Status of Executive Orders January 8, 1937 - Present

[2] Archives, National. (2012, July 11). Federal Register, What is the Electoral College? Retrieved July 11, 2012

WHEN DID "LOBBY" BECOME A FOUR LETTER WORD?

L obbying is a dirty word.

Ask anyone. Read the paper. Watch TV. Listen to talk radio. For the past few years, every time I heard about political influence and lobbying, there was a prevailing view that if we just got rid of the Washington lobbyists, everything would be fine.

But is this possible or even desirable? Is it what we really want?

I don't think so.

According to the First Amendment of the US Constitution "Congress shall make no law respecting an establishment of religion, or prohibiting the free exercise thereof; or abridging the freedom of speech, or of the press; or the right of the people peaceably to assemble, and to petition the Government for a redress of grievances." [1]

Apparently, the founders were troubled by King George III's inability to listen to polite criticism.

Basically, the Constitution gives us not only the right to talk to our representative but encourages us to appeal to them, to persuade them, to convince them to our point of view, i.e., to lobby. The First Amendment guarantees it.

We're doing it every day with our spouse anyway, with our roommates, our co-workers, and our boss. So why do we have such a problem with lobbying?

For most of us, I think we feel that it is unfairly applied -- meaning that it's only the big guys and the special interests that actually make their views known to Congress. This is generally true.

But that's not their fault. It's ours.

In the last 10 years, the lobbying industry has doubled in size and grown into a $3.5B per year business with about 10,000 lobbyists,[2], and that's just at the federal level.

We, the silent majority (I include myself in this group) have been conditioned to believe that if we vote for a representative every few years that will be good enough. We'll get what we want. We now know that's a myth.

Occasionally the literary, the erudite, and brave ones among us write a letter to our Congressman, to the editor of our local newspaper or the New York Times. Some of us sign petitions, make campaign contributions, or even go out and protest.

But does that get the job done? Sometimes it does.

Personally, I'd like to believe that one brilliant, well-written letter to my Congressman with a friendly follow-up phone call to their Legislative Director would be enough to get him or her to change their opinion about a pending law. But out of the almost 700,000 constituents[3] in my congressional district, there are likely a handful of people who would take the exact opposite position of me.

Sometimes they have more money, more time on their hands and they're more eloquent than I am. If they work for a large corporation with a PAC or are a union member, they seem to have a more significant political advantage to getting their views in front of my Congressman and often make more of an impression then I can alone as an individual.

I should just give up, right? Let someone else decide what's right for me.

Perhaps.

So is that why "lobby" has become a four-letter word?

If I can't lobby, don't let anyone else do it either. If I can't effectively persuade my representative, no one else should either. We should just rely on the ballot box.

But The Economist recently pointed out that "As this direct democracy" and its consequence "ballot-box budgeting," have grown representative democracy (i.e., the legislature) has become dysfunctional... California suffers from the same hyper-partisan and acrimonious deadlock between Republicans and Democrats as Washington does." [4]

You and I have the right to petition our government for grievances and express our point of view. In all likelihood, I'm not really sure that my point of view is going to be heard or even taken into account. Don't ask me why. It's just how I feel.

Sometimes I wondered if other people thought the way I do.

So I started asking around at the Little League, soccer practice, Boy Scouts and Brownies and to other parents at our children's school and once we got past the "Oh, it's okay to talk about politics." part, I found that for the most part everyone seemed really frustrated by the political process. I was in good company.

These were just average people; teachers, lawyers, barbers, car salesmen, repairmen, and a few VCs. No matter who it was, they really believed that if they voted and got "their" candidate into office, then we would have a panacea for this nasty problem of highly paid lobbyists controlling the agenda.

Everything would be wonderful again.

But deep in their hearts, they suspected that their singular voice did not matter and so often resigned themselves to saying, "But what can you do? There's nothing you can do."

Personally, I doubt if this is true because I think our representative has a point of view about what issues are important to her, what side of the argument she stands on and what she would and would not vote for and support. She would welcome hearing from her constituents either directly or indirectly.

That's why we have a representative democratic republic. We elect our representatives, and they make decisions. Got it?

They don't do what you want. They do what they want. The only thing you can do is vote them out and get somebody else in.

But why wait two years before we have a conversation with them?

Have our apathy, focus, and daily distractions kept us away from debate on the real issues?

If we evaluated our employees and spoke to our spouse once every two years, we wouldn't have a job or a marriage. The dialog needs to be persistent, focused, and fact-based.

I think members of Congress are pretty much realists and political animals. They understand that to pass legislation, they have to convince half of the House or Senate to agree with them on key points. So your Congressman is always involved in coalition-building no matter what the issue is. He is trying to persuade his peers to get them to agree with him every day he is in office.

This act of persuading or trying to bring him around to my point of view then is really an appeal on my part and is, in fact, lobbying. I am trying to convince him to think the way I do, believe what I do, and therefore vote the way I would like him to vote.

The frustrating part for all of us is that our representatives don't always vote the way we want.

Someone persuading someone else or lobbying someone is not a terrible thing. So, we shouldn't get rid of it.

Effective lobbying is pure salesmanship. There are good salespeople and bad ones. They inform us about products and services. From them, we ultimately learn the distinctions, comparisons, and differences among a wide variety of choices. Products or politics, it's all the same.

Lobbyists educate our legislators. If they appear to have too much power, it's only because we have taken a backseat and allowed a representative democracy to take place where we are not actively engaged anymore.

We have taken ourselves out of the political debate, and we spend our time in our apolitical routine.

Consider the persistently high ratings for Americas Got Talent[5] versus political news briefings.

If we can bring ourselves together, we could take charge and have a voice in the political arena. We could pool our resources and have as much clout as a top lobbyist.

What separates us from the activity of lobbyists?

THREE CRITICAL THINGS:

1. Clarity of message
2. A critical mass of constituents who believe in the same thing
3. Consistency of financial support for the issue and the persistence to follow through

WITH THESE THREE ELEMENTS, we too, can shape our political destiny.

Am I describing political Utopia?

No. I am merely describing a crowd-sourced funding platform for personal persuasion. This would enable the silent majority to debate and express their views.

Voting is essential, but having a consistent dialog with our representatives between elections should not be set aside.

This way, you do not have to stand in the street on a rainy night waiting for the media to feature you on the 6 o'clock news to gain attention for your burning issue. Those days are over.

You don't have to sit in your public affairs office, wondering how you are going to locate 10,000 supporters outside your district. You do not have to sign petitions that you don't understand, nor wonder if your campaign contribution is enough to help gain you access to your representative.

You don't have to act in isolation anymore. The technological and practical means for political change are here today.

You can come together to shape your future without quitting your day job.

If we act in unison on critical issues, I believe that we would turn "lobby" from a four-letter pejorative word into a statement of personal power.

-----

[1] US Congress. (n.d.). Amendments to the Constitution Article I. Retrieved 07 04, 2012, from US House of Representatives

[2] Politics, C. f. (2012, June 19). Open Secrets. Retrieved from OpenSecrets.org Lobbying Database

[3] Census, US. (2010, April 1). US Census 2010. Retrieved from Apportionment Data

[4] The Economist. (2012, June 16). California, Not Quite Greek But Still Weak. The Economist

[5] Ratings, Nielsen. (2012, June 18). Television Prime Broadcast Network TV - United States Week of June 18, 2012. Retrieved from Top 10 TV Ratings | Top 10 TV Shows

REVIEW

If you liked this book, please fee free to leave an honest review. Just a line or two would be very helpful. I want you to know that I will definitely read your review. Thanks so much. Here are the links.

Policy Snacks

US

http://www.amazon.com/review/create-review?&asin=B07DT36TYC

Goodreads

https://www.goodreads.com/review/new/40594368-policy-snacks

Author's Direct Audio Book

https://shop.authors-direct.com/products/policy-snacks-noshing-your-way-to-political-success?_pos=1&_sid=1610944b4&_ss=r

Preview: If you are frustrated by politics, and you don't think there's a way to make a difference, learn how there is an easier and productive way. Don't over complicate it and no need to be a political science major to get started. Find the way for you to move your issue forward and begin to improve your community, influence the country, and impact the world.

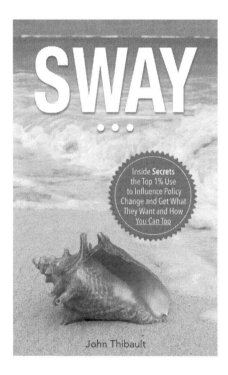

Frustrated voters now have an alternative way to make decisions. We want to revolutionize voting and simplify how bills and laws are created. Sway gives the reader a quick overview of the process that you can use to fix broken laws and improve the world. Learn the tools and network you will need to begin to fund your solution.

ABOUT THE AUTHOR

John Thibault is an award winning author and the founder and CEO of Silicon Valley startup, iLobby. He wrote the #1 International best-seller, "How to Change a Law," "Sway," and "The Political Game."

Previously he served in government affairs at MCA/Universal. He was also the first VP of business development and marketing at eBay and the first VP of marketing at Financial Engines.

He has been published in Association News, Manufacturing Today, CEO for High Growth Ventures and Millennial Magazine, and been interviewed on Amazon TV, and numerous radio affiliates for ABC, CBS, and NBC, podcasts and recently served on a panel for the "Tales of the Cocktail" Foundation.

He holds a Bachelor's degree from Ryerson University and an MFA from UCLA. He is a two-time cancer survivor, enjoys skiing and lives with his wife and three children in Northern California.

"If you've found this book useful, please consider leaving a short review."

f facebook.com/ilobby.co
🐦 twitter.com/ajohnthibault
a amazon.com/author/johnthibault
g goodreads.com/John_Thibault

ABOUT ILOBBY

iLobby is an online platform that makes it easy for voters, small businesses, and trade associations to take political action by engaging in public policy.

iLobby connects voters with lobbyists to change laws.

People use iLobby to debate issues, seek resolution to political problems in the world or their community, and to discover, share, and express what is important to them.

facebook.com/ilobby.co

twitter.com/ilobbyco

AWARDS

How To Change a Law

- **Gold Medal Winner**, Readers' Favorite Awards, 2017
- **Finalist,** 14th Annual American Book Fest, 2017
- Finalist, 11th Annual National Indie Excellence Book Awards, 2017
- Runner-Up, San Francisco Book Festival, 2017

iLobby

- **Finalist**, Community of Democracies "Annual Democracy Contest," 2016 Warsaw, Poland
- Quarterfinalist, Pepperdine University Most Fundable Companies, 2020

BONUS LINKS

- Web
- Twitter
- Twitter 2
- Facebook
- Blog
- Linked In
- Medium
- Instagram
- Quora
- YouTube
- iTunes Podcast
- Free Online Course
- Email Us

～

FREE STUFF

- 6 Things Politicians Want to Know
- 6 Reasons Why Congress Won't Listen To You
- Chet Campanella Story
- Free Online Interactive Course

Visit http://www.ilobbyco.com

~

SHARE YOUR STORY

If you have a story about how you changed a law, we would love to read it. It could be at the local, state or any level of government. We just ask that it be true, personal, and please keep it under 1200 words.

If your story is accepted, we may include it in a future version of How to Change a Law. Readers find these stories empowering, and it helps them believe that they can make a difference.

Simply email it to us with your contact information to support@ilobbyco.com

Please do not be discouraged if you do not hear back from us right away, as this can take time. If you do not hear from us within 90 days, chances are it is not right for us at this time.

Made in the USA
Middletown, DE
21 March 2024